To you —
A dear blessing
& God's gift in my life
May the weekly bless you all
& be one with you
In JMJ.

A Special Gift

For

From

Date

Message

Rainbow

of

Blessings

~ Helen Steiner Rice ~

Fleming H. Revell
A Division of Baker Book House Co
Grand Rapids, Michigan 49516

RAINBOW OF BLESSINGS

© 1997: Christian Art, P O Box 1599, Vereeniging, 1930, South Africa

Designed by: Christian Art

ISBN 0-8007-7169-9

Printed in Singapore

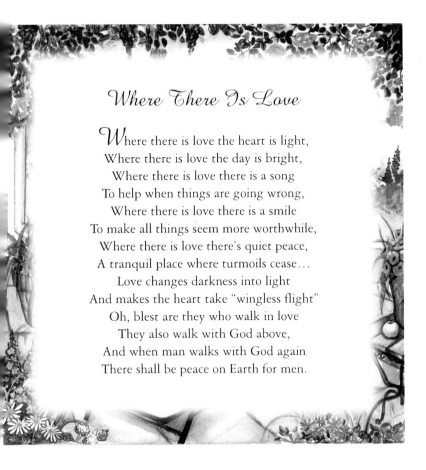

Where There Is Love

Where there is love the heart is light,
Where there is love the day is bright,
Where there is love there is a song
To help when things are going wrong,
Where there is love there is a smile
To make all things seem more worthwhile,
Where there is love there's quiet peace,
A tranquil place where turmoils cease…
Love changes darkness into light
And makes the heart take "wingless flight"
Oh, blest are they who walk in love
They also walk with God above,
And when man walks with God again
There shall be peace on Earth for men.

"In Him We Live, And Move, And Have Our Being"

We walk in a world that is strange and unknown
And in the midst of the crowd we still feel alone,
We question our purpose, our part, and our place
In this vast land of mystery suspended in space,
We probe and explore and try hard to explain
The tumult of thoughts that our minds entertain ...
But all of our probings and complex explanations
Of man's inner feelings and fears and frustrations
Still leave us engulfed in the "mystery of life"
With all of its struggles and suffering and strife,
Unable to fathom what tomorrow will bring –
But there is one truth to which we can cling,
For while life's a mystery man can't understand
The Great Giver of life is holding our hand
And safe in His care there is no need for seeing
For "in Him we live, and move, and have our being".

He Loves You!

It's amazing and incredible,
But it's as true as it can be,
God loves and understands us all
And that means *you* and *me* –
His grace is all sufficient
For both the young and old,
For the lonely and the timid,
For the brash and for the bold –
His love knows no exceptions,
So never feel excluded,
No matter *who* or *what* you are
Your name has been included –
And no matter what your past has been,
Trust God to understand,
And no matter what your problem is
Just place it in His hand –
For in all of our unloveliness
This great God loves us still,
He loved us since the world began
And what's more, *He always will!*

What More Can You Ask

God's love endureth forever —
What a wonderful thing to know
When the tides of life run against you
And your spirit is downcast and low ...

God's kindness is ever around you,
Always ready to freely impart
Strength to your faltering spirit,
Cheer to your lonely heart ...

God's presence is ever beside you,
As near as the reach of your hand,
You have but to tell Him your troubles,
There is nothing He won't understand ...

And knowing God's love is unfailing,
And His mercy unending and great,
You have but to trust in His promise –
'God comes not too soon or too late" ...

So wait with a heart that is patient
For the goodness of God to prevail –
For never do prayers go unanswered,
And His mercy and love never fail.

Nothing On Earth Is Forever Yours — Only The Love Of The Lord Endures!

Everything in life is passing
      and whatever we possess
Cannot endure forever
      but ends in nothingness,
For there are no safety boxes
      nor vaults that can contain
The possessions we collected
      and desire to retain ...
So all that man acquires,
      be it power, fame, or jewels,
Is but limited and earthly,
      only "treasure made for fools" ...
For only in God's Kingdom
      can man find enduring treasure,

Priceless gifts of love and beauty –
more than mortal man can measure,
And the "riches" he accumulates
he can keep and part with never,
For only in God's Kingdom
do our treasures last *forever* ...
So use the word *forever*
with sanctity and love,
For nothing is forever
but the *love of God above!*

Listen In Silence If You Would Hear

Silently the green leaves grow
In silence falls the soft, white snow
Silently the flowers bloom
In silence sunshine fills a room
Silently bright stars appear
In silence velvet night draws near ...
And silently God enters in
To free a troubled heart from sin
For God works silently in lives
For nothing spiritual survives
Amid the din of a noisy street
Where raucous crowds with hurrying feet
And "blinded eyes" and "deafened ear"
Are never privileged to hear
The message God wants to impart
To every troubled, weary heart
For only in a quiet place
Can man behold God *face to face!*

Talk It Over With God

You're worried and troubled
  about everything,
Wondering and fearing
  what tomorrow will bring –
You long to tell someone
  for you feel so alone,
But your friends are all burdened
  with cares of their own –
There is only one place
  and only One Friend
Who is never too busy
  and you can always depend
That He will be waiting
  with arms open wide
To hear all your troubles
  that you came to confide –
For the heavenly Father
  will always be there
When you seek Him and find Him
  at the *altar of prayer*.

Are You Dissatisfied With Yourself?

We are often discontented
　　　　and much dissatisfied
That our wish for recognition
　　　　has not been gratified.
We feel that we've been cheated
　　　　in beauty, charm, and brains
And we think of all our "losses"
　　　　and forget all about our "gains",
And dwelling on the things we lack
　　　　we grow miserable inside,
Brooding on our "deficits"
　　　　that are born of selfish pride.
We begin to harbor hatred
　　　　and envy fills our heart
That we do not possess the things
　　　　that make others "seem so smart".

And in our condemnation
    of the traits that we possess
We magnify our painful plight
    and sink deeper in distress.
Oh, Lord, forgive our foolishness,
    our vanity, and pride
As we strive to please the eye of man
    and not God who sees *"inside"*.
And little do we realize
    how contented we would be
If we knew that we were *beautiful*
    when our hearts are touched by Thee!

Prayers Can't Be Answered Unless They Are Prayed

*L*ife without purpose is barren indeed –
There can't be a harvest unless you plant seed,
There can't be attainment unless there's a goal,
And man's but a robot unless there's a soul ...
If we send no ships out, no ships will come in,
And unless there's a contest, nobody can win ...
For games can't be won unless they are played,
And prayers can't be answered unless they are *prayed* ...
So whatever is wrong with your life today,
You'll find a solution if you kneel down and pray
Not just for pleasure, enjoyment and health,
Not just for honors and prestige and wealth ...
But pray for a purpose to make life worth living,
And pray for the joy of unselfish giving,
For great is your gladness and rich your reward
When you make your *life's purpose* the choice of the Lord.

"This Too Will Pass Away"

If I can endure for this minute
Whatever is happening to me,
No matter how heavy my heart is
Or how "dark" the moment may be –
If I can remain calm and quiet
With all my world crashing about me,
Secure in the knowledge God loves me
When everyone else seems to doubt me –
If I can but keep on believing
What I know in my heart to be true,
That "darkness will fade with the morning"
And that this will pass away, too –
Then nothing in life can defeat me
For as long as this knowledge remains
I can suffer whatever is happening
For I know God will break "all the chains"
That are binding me tight in "the darkness"
And trying to fill me with fear –
For there is no night without dawning
And I know that "my morning" is near.

When Trouble Comes
And Things Go Wrong!

Let us go quietly to God
        when troubles come to us,
Let us never stop to whimper
        or complain and fret and fuss,
Let us hide "our thorns" in "roses"
        and our sighs in "golden song"
And "our crosses" in a "crown of smiles"
        whenever things go wrong ...
For no one can really help us
        as our troubles we bemoan,
For comfort, help and inner peace
        must come from God alone ...
Do not tell you neighbor,
        your companion or your friend
In the hope that they can help you
        bring your troubles to an end ...

for they, too, have their problems,
      they are burdened just like you,
so take your cross to Jesus
      and He will see you through ...
and waste no time in crying
      on the shoulder of a friend
but go directly to the Lord
      for on Him you can depend ...
for there's absolutely *nothing*
      that His mighty hand can't do
and He never is too busy
      to help and comfort you.

People's Problems

Everyone has problems
        in this restless world of care,
Everyone grows weary
        with the "cross they have to bear",
Everyone is troubled
        and "their skies are overcast"
As they try to face the future
        while still dwelling in the past.
But the people with their problems
        only "listen with one ear",
For people only listen
        to the things they want to hear
And they only hear the kind of things
        they are able to believe

l's to give
·eceive,
۱s
day
them
۱l way.
es,
۱ntly
To   olems
be –
So may the people of all nations
    at last become aware
That God will solve the peoples' problems
    through *faith* and *hope* and *prayer!*

Life's Bitterest Disappointments Are God's Sweetest Appointments

Out of life's misery born of man's sins
A fuller, richer life begins,
For when we are helpless with no place to go
And our hearts are heavy and our spirits are low,
If we place our poor, broken lives in God's hands
And surrender completely to His Will and demands,
The "darkness lifts" and the "sun shines through"
And by His touch we are "born anew" ...
So praise God for trouble that "cuts like a knife"
And disappointments that shatter your life,
For with *patience* to wait and *faith* to endure
Your life will be blessed and your future secure,
For God is but testing your faith and your love
Before He "appoints you" to rise far above
All the small things that so sorely distress you,
For God's only intention is to strengthen and bless you.

How Great The Yield
From A Fertile Field

The farmer plows through the fields of green
And the blade of the plow is sharp and keen,
But the seed must be sown to bring forth grain,
For nothing is born without suffering and pain –
And God never plows in the soul of man
Without intention and purpose and plan,
So whenever you feel the plow's sharp blade
Let not your heart be sorely afraid
For, like the farmer, God chooses a field
From which He expects an excellent yield –
So rejoice though your heart is broken in two,
God seeks to bring forth a rich harvest in you.

Why Am I Complaining?

My cross is not too heavy,
My road is not too rough
Because God walks beside me
And to know this is enough ...
And though I get so lonely
I know I'm not alone
For the Lord God is my Father
And He loves me as His own ...
So though I'm tired and weary
And I wish my race were run

od will only terminate it
my work on earth is done ...
let me stop complaining
bout my "load of care"
God will always lighten it
n it gets too much to bear ...
f He does not ease my load
ill give me strength to bear it
For God in love and mercy
Is always near to share it.

It Takes The Bitter And The Sweet To Make A Life Full And Complete

Life is a mixture
     of sunshine and rain,
Laughter and teardrops,
     pleasure and pain –
Low tides and high tides,
     mountains and plains.
Triumphs, defeats
     and losses and gains –
But *always* in *all ways*
     God's guiding and leading

And He alone knows
        the things we're most needing –
And when He sends sorrow
        or some dreaded affliction.
Be assured that it comes
        with God's kind benediction –
And if we accept it
        as a gift of His Love.
We'll be showered with blessings
        from our Father above.

Dark Shadows Fall In The Lives Of Us All

Sickness and sorrow
    come to us all,
But through it we grow
    and learn to "stand tall" –
For trouble is part
    and parcel of life
And no man can grow
    without struggle and strife,
And the more we endure
    with patience and grace

The stronger we grow
and the more we can face –
And the more we can face,
the greater our love,
And with love in our hearts
we are more conscious of
The pain and the sorrow
in lives everywhere,
So it is through trouble
that we learn how to share.

Prayers Are The Stairs To God

Prayers are the stairs
We must climb every day,
If we would reach God
There is no other way,
For we learn to know God
When we meet Him in prayer
And ask Him to lighten
Our burden of care –
So start in the morning
And though the way's steep,
Climb ever upward
Till your eyes close in sleep –
For prayers are the stairs
That lead to the Lord,
And to meet Him in prayer
Is the climber's reward.

Let Not Your Heart Be Troubled

Whenever I am troubled
　　　　and lost in deep despair
bundle all my troubles up
　　　　and go to God in prayer ...
tell Him I am heartsick
　　　　and lost and lonely, too,
That my mind is deeply burdened
　　　　and I don't know what to do ...
But I know He stilled the tempest
　　　　and calmed the angry sea
And I humbly ask if in His love
　　　　He'll do the same for me ...
And then I just keep quiet
　　　　and think only thoughts of peace
and if I abide in stillness
　　　　my "restless murmurings" cease.

God, Grant Me The Glory Of "Thy Gift"

God, widen my vision so I may see
the afflictions You have sent to me –
Not as a cross too heavy to wear
that weighs me down in gloomy despair –
Not as something to hate and despise
but a gift of love sent in disguise –
Something to draw me closer to You
to teach me patience and forbearance, too –
Something to show me more clearly the way
to *serve* You and *love* You more every day –
Something priceless and precious and rare
that will keep me forever safe in Thy care
Aware of the spiritual strength that is mine
if my selfish, small will is lost in Thine!

The Soul Of Man

Every man has a deep heart need
That cannot be filled with doctrine
or creed,
For the soul of man knows nothing more
Than just that he is longing for
A haven that is safe and sure,
A fortress where he feels secure,
An island in this sea of strife,
Away from all the storms of life ...
Oh, God of love, who sees us all,
You are so Great! We are so small!
Hear man's universal prayer
Crying to you in despair –
"Save my soul and grant me peace,
Let my restless murmurings cease,
God of love, forgive! forgive!
Teach me how to truly live ...
Ask me not my race or creed
Just take me in my hour of need
Let me feel You love me, too,
And that I am a part of You".

He Was One Of Us

He was born as little children are
and lived as children do,
So remember that the Saviour
was once a Child like you,
And remember that He lived on earth
in the midst of sinful men,
And the problems of the present
existed even then;
He was ridiculed and laughed at
in the same heartbreaking way
That we who fight for justice
are ridiculed today;
He was tempted ... He was hungry ...
He was lonely ... He was sad ...
There's no sorrowful experience
that the Saviour has not had;
And in the end He was betrayed
and even crucified,

For He was truly "One of Us" –
He lived on earth and died;
So do not heed the skeptics
who are often heard to say:
"What does God up in Heaven
know of things we face today" ...
For, our Father up in heaven
is very much aware
Of our failures and shortcomings
and the burdens that we bear,
So whenever you are troubled
put your problems in God's Hand
For He has faced all problems
and He will understand.

On The Wings Of Prayer

Just close your eyes and open your heart
And feel your worries and cares depart,
Just yield yourself to the Father above
And let Him hold you secure in His love –
For life on earth grows more involved
With endless problems that can't be solved –
But God only asks us to do our best,
Then He will "take over" and finish the rest –
So when you are tired, discouraged and blue,
There's always one door that is open to you –

And that is the door to "the House of Prayer"
And you'll find God waiting to meet you there,
And "the House of Prayer" is no farther away
Than the quiet spot where you kneel and pray –
For the heart is a temple when God is there
As we place ourselves in His loving care,
And He hears every prayer and answers each one
When we pray in His Name "Thy will be done" –
And the burdens that seemed too heavy to bear
Are lifted away on "the Wings of Prayer".

Thank You, God, For Everything

Thank you, God, for everything – the big things and the small,
For "every good gift comes from God" – the Giver of them all –
And all too often we accept without any thanks or praise
The gifts God sends as blessings each day in many ways –
First, thank you for the little things that often come our way,
The things we take for granted but don't mention when we pray,
Then, thank you for the "miracles" we are much too blind to see,
And give us new awareness of our many gifts from Thee,
And help us to remember that the key to Life and Living
Is to make each prayer a prayer of thanks and every day Thanksgiving.

Every Day Is A Holiday To Thank And Praise The Lord

Special poems for special seasons
are meaningful indeed,
But daily inspiration
is still man's greatest need –
For day by day all through the year,
not just on holidays,
Man should glorify the Lord
in deeds and words of praise –
And when the heart is heavy
and everything goes wrong,
May these "Daily Words for Daily Needs"
be like a cheery song
Assuring you "He loves you"
and that "you never walk alone" –
For in God's all-wise wisdom
your every need is known!

Look On The Sunny Side

There are always two sides, the good and the bad,
The dark and the light, the sad and the glad –
But in looking back over the good and the bad
We're aware of the number of good things we've had –
And in counting our blessings we find when we're through
We've no reason at all to complain or be blue –
So thank God for good things He has already done,
And be grateful to Him for the battles you've won,
And know that the same God who helped you before
Is ready and willing to help you once more –
Then with faith in your heart reach out for God's Hand
And accept what He sends, though you can't understand –
For our Father in heaven always knows what is best,
And if you trust in His wisdom your life will be blest,
For always remember that whatever betide you,
You are never alone for God is beside you.

Never Borrow Sorrow From Tomorrow

Deal only with the present,
Never step into tomorrow,
For God asks us just to trust Him
And to never borrow sorrow –
For the future is not ours to know
And it may never be,
So let us live and give our best
And give it lavishly –
For to meet tomorrow's troubles
Before they are even ours
Is to anticipate the Saviour
And to doubt His all-wise powers –
So let us be content to solve
Our problems one by one,
Asking nothing of tomorrow
Except "Thy will be done".

Be Of Good Cheer—
There's Nothing To Fear!

Cheerful thoughts like sunbeams
Lighten up the "darkest fears"
For when the heart is happy
There's just no time for tears —
And when the face is smiling
It's impossible to frown
And when you are "high-spirited"
You cannot feel "low-down" —
For the nature of our attitude
Toward circumstantial things
Determines our acceptance
Of the problems that life brings.
And since fear and dread and worry
Cannot help in any way,
It's much healthier and happier

To be cheerful every day –
And if you'll only try it
You will find, without a doubt,
A cheerful attitude's something
No one should be without –
For when the heart is cheerful
It cannot be filled with fear.
And without fear the way ahead
Seems more distinct and clear –
And we realize there's nothing
We need ever face alone
For our Heavenly Father loves us
And our problems are His own.

Worry No More! God Knows The Score!

Have you ever been caught
     in a web you didn't weave,
Involved in conditions
     that are hard to believe?
Have you felt you must speak
     and explain and deny
A story that's groundless
     or a small, whispered lie?
Have you ever heard rumors
     you would like to refute
Or some telltale gossip
     you would like to dispute?
Well, don't be upset
     for God knows the score
And with God as your judge
     you need worry no more,
For men may misjudge you
     but God's verdict is fair

For He looks deep inside
      and He is clearly aware
Of every small detail
      in your pattern of living
And always He's lenient
      and fair and forgiving –
And knowing that God
      is your judge and your jury
Frees you completely
      from man's falseness and fury,
And secure in this knowledge
      let your thoughts rise above
Man's small, shallow judgments
      that are so empty of
God's Goodness and Greatness
      in judging all men
And forget "ugly rumors"
      and be happy again.

Yesterday ... Today ...
And Tomorrow!

Yesterday's dead,
Tomorrow's unborn,
So there's nothing to fear
And nothing to mourn,
For all that is past
And all that has been
Can never return
To be lived once again –
And what lies ahead
Or the things that will be
Are still in God's Hands
So it is not up to me
To live in the future
That is God's great unknown,
for the past and the present
God claims for His own,

o all I need do
s to live for today
And trust God to show me
The truth and the way –
For it's only the memory
Of things that have been
And expecting tomorrow
To bring trouble again
That fills my today,
Which God wants to bless,
With uncertain fears
And borrowed distress –
For all I need live for
Is this one little minute,
For life's here and now
And eternity's in it.

"I Am The Way, The Truth, And The Life"

I am the *Way*
so just follow Me
Though the way be rough
and you cannot see …

I am the *Truth*
which all men seek
So heed not "false prophets"
nor the words that they speak …

I am the *Life*
and I hold the key
That opens the door
to eternity …

And in this dark world
I am the *Light*
To the Promised Land
Where there is no night!